FLANNE
LAZY
COOKBOOK

“Slow Cooker, Crock Pot and Dutch Oven Recipes”

Second Edition

By Tim Murphy

For information on Flannel John’s Cookbooks for Guys, upcoming releases and merchandise visit www.flanneljohn.com

FLANNEL JOHN'S LAZY GUY COOKBOOK

"Slow Cooker, Crock Pot & Dutch Oven Recipes"

TABLE OF CONTENTS

ALL-DAY STEW

1½ pounds of beef, venison or elk, cubed
1 can of cream of mushroom soup
2 cans of golden mushroom soup
6 carrots, chopped
1 cup of celery, chopped
4 potatoes, chopped
1 package of Lipton's Onion Soup mix

Put ingredients in a cooker, cover and cook on low for 8 to 10 hours.

APPLESAUCE

10 apples, peeled, cored and sliced
½ cup of water
½ cup of sugar
½ cup of brown sugar
2 tablespoons of cinnamon
1 teaspoon of nutmeg
½ teaspoon of ground cloves
1 tablespoon of butter
2 tablespoons of lemon juice

Place ingredients in the cooker and stir thoroughly. Cover and cook on low for 8 to 10 hours. Chill the sauce upon completion or spoon the warm mixture on vanilla ice cream.

BACON CHEESE DIP

1 pound of bacon, diced
1 pound of cream cheese, softened and cubed
4 cups of Cheddar cheese, shredded
1 cup of half & half
2 teaspoons of Worcestershire sauce
1 teaspoon of dried onion, minced
½ teaspoon of dry mustard
½ teaspoon of salt
Tabasco sauce to taste (optional)

Brown bacon in a pan, drain and set aside. Put remaining ingredients in the cooker, cover and cook on low for 1 hour stirring occasionally until cheese is completely melted. Stir in bacon and cook for a few more minutes.

BAKED CHICKEN

3 pounds of chicken pieces
1 teaspoon of paprika
Salt and pepper

Make three 3-inch balls of aluminum foil and place them at the bottom of the crock-pot. Place chicken on top of the foil. Sprinkle with salt, pepper and paprika. Cover and cook on high for 1 hour, then switch to low for 8 to 10 hours.

BAKED OATMEAL

2 cups of dry quick oats
½ cup of sugar
1 egg, beaten
1½ teaspoons of baking powder
½ teaspoon of salt
¾ cup of milk
¼ cup of oil

Pour oil into the cooker to coat the bottom and sides. Add ingredients into the cooker and mix thoroughly. Cover and bake on low for 2½ to 3 hours.

BANANA BREAD

¾ cup of butter or margarine
1½ cups of sugar
1½ cups of mashed banana
½ cup of milk
2 eggs beaten
2 cups of flour
1 teaspoon of baking soda
¾ teaspoon of salt
½ cup walnuts, chopped (optional)

Combine ingredients and mix well to make a batter. Pour the batter into a greased and floured clean coffee can or similar metal container. Fill the container 2/3 full with batter. Make sure it fits loosely in the cooker. Cover the top of the can with 4 paper towels. Do not put water in the cooker. Put can in the cooker and put the lid on the cooker. Make sure the lid is slightly askew so excess moisture can escape. Cook on high for 4 hours.

BARBECUED CHICKEN

2 pounds of chicken pieces
2 cups of water
1 cup of ketchup
¼ cup of flour
¼ cup of Worcestershire sauce
1 teaspoon of chili powder
½ teaspoon of salt
½ teaspoon of pepper
¼ teaspoon of garlic salt
¼ teaspoon of onion salt
Tabasco sauce to taste

Dust the chicken pieces with flour and place in the cooker. Combine the rest of the ingredients in a bowl, mix thoroughly and pour over chicken. Pout the cover on and cook on low for 5 hours.

BARBECUED GAME STEAK

2 pounds of venison or elk steak
1 cup of water
3 tablespoons of oil
1 cup of onion, diced
¾ cup of ketchup
½ cup of vinegar
½ cup of brown sugar
1 tablespoon of mustard
1 tablespoon of Worcestershire sauce
½ teaspoon of salt
¼ teaspoon of pepper

Cut steak into pieces and place into Dutch oven with oil. Heat and brown meat on both sides. Remove the meat, add onion and brown. Add remaining ingredients to make the sauce, cover and simmer for 5 minutes. Return meat to the pot and bake for 2 hours or until steak is tender.

BARBECUED HAM

2 pounds of ham, cubed
2 cups of cola
2 cups of ketchup

Place ham in the cooker and pour cola and ketchup over the meat. Cover and cook on low for 8 hours. Serve on hamburger or hot dog buns.

BARBECUED HOT DOGS

2 pounds of hot dogs, cut into 1-inch pieces
1 cup of apricot preserves
4 ounces of tomato sauce
¼ cup of vinegar
2 tablespoons of soy sauce
2 tablespoons of honey
1 tablespoon of oil
1 teaspoon of salt
¼ teaspoon of fresh ground ginger

Combine all of the ingredients in the cooker except the hot dogs. Stir, cover and cook on high for 30 minutes. Add hot dogs and reduce heat to low. Cover and cook for 4 hours.

BARBECUED RIBLETS

4 pounds of country-style ribs,
  cut into bite-sized pieces
1 can of tomato soup
½ cup of apple cider vinegar
½ cup of brown sugar
1 tablespoon of soy sauce
1 teaspoon of celery seed
1 teaspoon of salt
1 teaspoon of chili powder
Cayenne pepper to taste

Place ribs in the cooker. Mix remaining ingredients together thoroughly and pour over the meat. Cover and cook on low for 6 to 8 hours.

BEEF & GREEN BEANS

3 pounds of beef, cut into chunks
1 pound of frozen green beans
1 can of stewed tomatoes
1 onion, sliced into rings
1 tablespoon of paprika
1 tablespoon of Worcestershire sauce
1 teaspoon of garlic salt
1 teaspoon of garlic juice
Pepper to taste

Place ingredients in the cooker, cover and cook on low for 8 to 10 hours.

BEEF BARBECUE

4 pounds of lean beef, cut into chunks
14 ounces of tomatoes, canned
2 medium onions, diced
1 quart of water
1 cup of ketchup
1 tablespoon of chili powder
½ cup of vinegar
½ cup of Worcestershire sauce
Salt and pepper to taste
Garlic powder to taste
Liquid smoke (optional)
Hamburger buns

Combine all ingredients in a Dutch oven. Simmer uncovered on low heat for 5 to 6 hours or until beef falls to shreds. The mixture should be thick. Spoon onto hamburger buns.

BEEF ROAST

3 pound beef roast
1 envelope of dry onion soup mix
14 ounces of stewed tomatoes, canned

Put roast in the cooker and cover with onion soup and tomatoes. Cover and cook on low for 8 hours.

BEEF STEW

2 pounds of beef, cubed
3 potatoes, diced
1½ cups of beef broth
4 carrots, sliced
2 onions, diced
1 stalk of celery, diced
1 teaspoon of Worcestershire sauce
½ cup of flour
½ clove of garlic, minced
1½ teaspoons of salt
1 teaspoon of paprika
½ teaspoon of pepper
1 bay leaf

Place meat in the bottom of the cooker. Combine flour, salt, pepper and paprika and stir into the meat until all the cubes are coated. Add remaining ingredients and mix thoroughly. Cover and cook on low for 10 to 12 hours. Remove bay leaf before serving.

BEEF STROGANOFF

1 pound of round steak
1 cup of onions, diced
1 cup of beef broth
¼ cup of flour
8 ounces of mushrooms, canned or fresh
1 clove or garlic, minced
1 tablespoon of Dijon mustard
2 teaspoons of parsley
½ teaspoon of salt
¼ teaspoon of pepper
Egg noodles

Put steak, mushrooms, onion, mustard, dill, garlic, salt and pepper into the cooker. Mix beef broth and flour together. If mixture seems a little thin, add an additional teaspoon or two of flour. Pour the mixture into the cooker. Put on the cover and cook on low for 8 hours. Prepare noodles according to package directions and serve stroganoff over the noodles.

BEER BRATS

6 bratwurst, fresh not frozen
2 cloves or garlic, minced
2 tablespoons of olive oil
12 ounces of beer (1 can)

Brown meat in a pan with garlic and olive oil. Pierce casings of the sausages with a fork and cook for 5 more minutes. Put meat in the cooker and pour in the beer. Cover and cook on low for 6 to 7 hours.

BIG CHUNK O'BEEF

3 pounds of brisket or roast
4 potatoes, peeled and diced
4 carrots, cleaned and sliced
2 onions, diced
10 ounces of beef bouillon
1 cup of water
½ cup of red wine
2 tablespoons of parsley
1 tablespoon of Worcestershire sauce
2 teaspoons of salt
¼ teaspoon of pepper
1 bay leaf

Place vegetables in the cooker followed by meat, spices and liquid. Top with bay leaf so it's easy to remove after cooking. Cover and cook on low for 8 to 10 hours.

BIG GAME CHICKEN WINGS

5 pounds of chicken wings
28 ounces of tomato or spaghetti sauce
1 tablespoon of Worcestershire sauce
1 tablespoon of molasses
1 tablespoon of mustard
1 teaspoon of salt
½ teaspoon of pepper

Place wings in the cooker. Combine ingredients and pour over wings. Stir gently making sure each wing is coated. Cover and cook on high for 3 to 4 hours.

BOLOGNA & SAUERKRAUT

32-ounce bag of sauerkraut, rinsed
1 large ring bologna
1/3 cup of brown sugar

Combine sauerkraut and brown sugar in the cooker and stir. Remove casing from bologna and cut into ¼-inch slices. Add to the sauerkraut and stir. Cover and cook on low for 6 to 8 hours.

BRUNSWICK STEW

1 pound of skinless, boneless chicken, diced
2 potatoes, sliced thin
1 can of tomato soup
16 ounces of stewed tomatoes, canned
10 ounces of frozen corn
10 ounces of frozen lima beans
3 tablespoons of onion flakes
¼ teaspoon of salt
Pepper to taste

Combine all the ingredients in the cooker. Cover and cook on high for 2 hours then reduce to low for 2 more hours.

CATFISH STEW

2 pounds of catfish fillets
6 slices of bacon
3 cups of potatoes, diced
1½ cups of onion, diced
28 ounces of canned tomatoes
8 ounces of tomato sauce
2 tablespoons of Worcestershire sauce
2 tablespoons of salt
Hot pepper sauce to taste (optional)
¼ teaspoon of pepper

Cut fresh or thawed catfish into 1 to 2 inch pieces. Fry bacon in the Dutch oven until crisp. Remove bacon and drain on paper towels, crumble and set aside. Add onion to the Dutch oven, cover and cook in bacon grease for 5 minutes or until tender. Add in all ingredients except catfish and crumbled bacon. Bring pot to a boil then simmer for 30 minutes. Add bacon and catfish, cover, and simmer for 8 to 10 minutes.

CHICKEN & MUSHROOMS

6 boneless, skinless chicken breast halves
1 can of cream of mushroom soup
4 ounces of sliced mushrooms,
(If using canned mushrooms, drain liquid)
¼ cup of chicken broth
Salt and pepper to taste

Place chicken in the cooker and season with salt and pepper. Combine chicken broth and soup and pour over chicken then top with mushrooms. Cover and cook on low for 7 to 9 hours.

CHICKEN GUMBO

2 pounds of boneless chicken breasts, cubed
2 pounds of okra, cut to ¼-inch slices
2 stalks of celery, diced
3 tomatoes, diced
2 onions, diced
2 bell peppers, diced
4 tablespoons of oil
3 tablespoons of flour
2 cloves of garlic, minced
1 quart of water
Salt and pepper to taste

Heat Dutch oven to 325 degrees and add oil and flour. Stir until flour browns. Add garlic, onion and bell peppers. Slowly stir in 1 quart of water. Add salt and pepper to taste followed by celery, okra and tomatoes. Heat to boiling then reduce to 225 degrees. Cover and simmer for 30 minutes and vegetables are cooked. Add chicken and simmer for another 20 minutes or until chicken is cooked.

CHICKEN POTATO CASSEROLE

1 chicken in parts
5 potatoes
1 can of cream of chicken soup
½ cup of green onions, chopped
½ can of water
Salt and pepper

Brown the chicken in a frying pan. In the Dutch oven, slice potatoes and salt and pepper to taste. Add green onions and place chicken on top. Mix soup with ½ can of water and pour over the top. Cover and bake for 60 to 90 minutes. Check during the last 30 minutes for doneness.

CHICKEN REUBEN POT

2 boneless, skinless chicken breasts
  cut in half
2 pounds of sauerkraut, rinsed and drained
4 slices of Swiss cheese
1¼ cups of Thousand Island salad dressing
2 tablespoons of fresh parsley, chopped

Put chicken in the cooker. Put sauerkraut over chicken and top with cheese. Pour salad dressing over the cheese and sprinkle with parsley. Cover and cook on low for 6 to 8 hours.

CHILI CHEESE DIP

1 pound of ground beef
½ cup of onion, diced
1 cup of Velveeta cheese, diced
5 ounces of tomatoes, diced
5 ounces of green chilies, diced
1 can of evaporated milk
Salt and pepper to taste

Brown ground beef in a pan with a little oil. Drain the grease and season with salt and pepper. Combine all the ingredients in the cooker, stir then cover. Set to low and cook for 4 hours. Stir every 45 minutes. This is the perfect dip for tailgating and football parties.

CHILI NUTS

24 ounces of canned cocktail peanuts
¼ cup of melted butter
Chili seasoning mix to taste

In the cooker, pour melted butter over the nuts. Sprinkle chili-seasoning mix over the nuts and toss. Cover and cook on low for 2 hours. Turn to high for 15 minutes. Remove lid and serve.

CHILI WITH BEANS

2 large cans of kidney beans, drained
2 pounds of ground beef
32 ounces of canned tomatoes
1 can of tomato paste
1 bell pepper, diced
1 onion, diced
3 tablespoons of chili powder
2 cloves of garlic, minced
Tabasco sauce to taste

Brown the meat in a skillet and drain. Add all ingredients to the slow cooker and stir. Cover and cook on low for 10 to 12 hours.

CLAM CHOWDER

30 ounces of cream of potato soup, canned
20 ounces of clam chowder, canned
12 ounces of canned clams, chopped
½ cup of butter
1 onion, diced
1 pint of half & half

Combine all the ingredients in the cooker. Cover and cook on low for 2 to 4 hours.

COLA BEEF

3 pounds of beef roast
24 ounces of cola (2 cans)
1 envelope of dry onion soup mix

Put roast in the cooker. Sprinkle with soup mix and pour cola all over the meat. Cover and cook on low for 7 to 8 hours.

COLA CHICKEN

4 boneless chicken breasts
1 can of cola
1 cup of ketchup
1 cup of barbecue sauce

Cut chicken breasts into strips. Mix cola, barbecue sauce and ketchup together in a Dutch oven. Heat to 350 degrees stirring continuously until it reaches that point. Drop in chicken strips and put on the lid. Cook for 45 minutes making sure to stir every 5 to 10 minutes. When chicken is done, serve on a bed of noodles or rice.

COLCANNON

6 potatoes, peeled and cubed
2 cups of cabbage, chopped
1 onion, diced
1 tablespoon of butter
½ teaspoon of salt
Pepper to taste
Water

Put potatoes in a Dutch oven and cover with water. Bring to a boil. Cover and cook over medium heat for 8 to 10 minutes, until potatoes are almost tender. Add cabbage and onion, cover and simmer for 5 minutes or until cabbage is tender. Drain well and mash with butter, salt and pepper.

CORNED BEEF

3 carrots, cleaned and chunked
3 pounds of corned beef brisket
2 onions, sliced into quarters
2 celery tops
1 turnip, sliced into chunks
3 potatoes, diced large

In the slow cooker, place layers of each ingredient in the order listed. Fill with water to about 1-inch from the top. Cover and cook on low for 8 to 10 hours.

CRAB SOUP

1 pound of crabmeat
1 pound of ham, diced
1 pound of beef, diced
6 slices of bacon, diced
1 pound of carrots, sliced
1 onion, diced
3 stalks of celery, diced
20 ounces of frozen mixed vegetables
12 ounces of tomato juice
1 tablespoon of Old Bay seasoning
1 teaspoon of salt
¼ teaspoon of pepper
Water

Put all ingredients in the cooker except crabmeat and seasonings. Pour in enough water so cooker is half-full. Add seasonings, stir thoroughly and put crab on top. Cover and cook on low for 8 to 10 hours. Stir well before serving.

CRANBERRY CHICKEN

3 pounds of chicken parts
16 ounces of cranberry sauce, berry not jelly
1 cup of barbecue sauce
½ cup of celery, diced
½ cup of onion, diced
½ teaspoon of salt
½ teaspoon of pepper

Put chicken in the cooker. Mix ingredients together thoroughly and pour over the parts. Cover and cook on low for 6 to 8 hours.

CREAMY RED POTATOES

2 pounds of small red potatoes, quartered
8 ounces of cream cheese, softened
1 10-ounce can of potato soup
1 package of dry Ranch salad dressing

Put potatoes in a slow cooker. Mix cream cheese, soup and Ranch dressing together and stir into potatoes. Cover and cook on low for 8 hour or until potatoes are tender.

CROCK-POT PIZZA

1 pound of Italian sausage,
browned, sliced and drained
28 ounces of tomatoes, diced
(canned or fresh)
16 ounces of chili beans, canned
2 ounces of canned black olives, chopped
1 medium onion, diced
1 green pepper, diced
2 cloves of garlic, minced
¼ cup of Parmesan cheese, grated
1 tablespoon of quick-cooking tapioca
1 tablespoon of basil
1 teaspoon of salt
Mozzarella cheese, shredded

Combine all ingredients in the cooker except mozzarella cheese. Stir thoroughly. Cover and cook on low for 8 to 9 hours. When serving, top with mozzarella cheese. Tastes great on pasta, rice or in a wrap.

DUTCH OVEN CAMP BREAKFAST

1 pound of venison, ground
2 tablespoons of oil
1 small onion, diced
12 eggs
1 can of diced chilies (choose your heat)
1 pound of cheddar cheese, shredded

Pour oil in a Dutch oven then brown venison and onion. Pour off excess grease and season to taste. Break eggs into oven and add chilies. Stir over medium heat until eggs are nearly cooked. Sprinkle cheese over the top. Remove from heat put on lid to let cheese melt for a few minutes.

ELK & KRAUT

3 potatoes, diced
1 ½ pounds of elk, ground
1 jar or can of sauerkraut, drained
 (12 to 16 ounces works)
1 cup of water
1 cup of croutons
1 onion, diced
1 egg, beaten
3 tablespoons of oil
2 tablespoons of brown sugar
2 tablespoons of salt
2 tablespoons of ketchup, barbecue sauce or
 chili sauce (choose to taste)
1 tablespoon of pepper

Heat oil in a Dutch oven. Add in all your ingredients and stir a few times. Put on the lid and leave it alone for 90 minutes to let the flavors blend. If cooking over a fire, too much heat will make the ingredients stick to the inside of the oven. Check for doneness after 90 minutes. If not cooked, check every 10 to 15 minutes.

GEORGIA RIBS

4 pounds of boneless pork ribs
15 ounces of canned spiced cling peaches, diced with juice
½ cup of brown sugar
¼ cup of ketchup
¼ cup of white vinegar
1 garlic clove, minced
2 tablespoons of soy sauce
1 teaspoon of salt
1 teaspoon of pepper

Cut ribs into bite-sized pieces. Brown in a pan with a little oil. Drain and put meat in the cooker. Combine remaining ingredients in a bowl and mix thoroughly. Pour over the ribs, cover and cook on low for 8 to 10 hours.

GLAZED CARROTS

2 pounds of baby carrots
½ cup of brown sugar
½ cup of fresh squeezed orange juice
3 tablespoons of butter
¾ teaspoon of cinnamon
¼ teaspoon of nutmeg
2 tablespoons of cornstarch
¼ cup of water

Combine all but the final 2 ingredients and place in a slow cooker. Cover and cook on low for 3 to 4 hours. Carrots should be tender but crisp, not mushy. Pour of the juice into a small pan. Put carrots in a baking dish. Bring juice to a boil and add the water and cornstarch mixture. Stir and boil for one minute until thick. Pour sauce over carrots in the baking dish.

GOURMET TOMATO SOUP

48 ounces of tomato juice
8 ounces of tomato sauce
½ cup of water
2 tablespoons of sugar
1 bouillon cube
1 tablespoon of chopped celery leaves
½ onion, thinly sliced
½ teaspoon of dried basil
½ teaspoon of whole cloves
1 bay leaf

Combine all ingredients in a lightly greased cooker and stir well. Cover and cook on low for 5 to 8 hours. Remove cloves and bay leaf before serving.

GRANDMA'S MINESTRONE

3 cups of water
1½ pounds of beef, venison or elk
1 onion, diced
4 carrots, sliced
14 ounces of canned tomatoes
10 ounces of frozen, mixed vegetables
1 tablespoon of basil
1 teaspoon of oregano
½ cup of vermicelli, uncooked

Combine all ingredients in the cooker and stir well. Cover and cook on low for 10 to 12 hours.

GREEK CHICKEN

5 potatoes, quartered
3 pounds of chicken parts
2 onions, quartered
1 bulb of garlic, minced
3 teaspoons of oregano
1 tablespoon of olive oil
1 teaspoon of salt
½ teaspoon of pepper

Put potatoes in the bottom of the cooker. Layer with chicken, onions and garlic. Sprinkle seasonings over everything. Drizzle with olive oil. Cover and cook on low for 9 to 10 hours.

HAM BONE SOUP

1 pound of dried navy beans
1 ham bone
6 cups of water

Soak beans overnight in 3 pints of water then drain. Put soaked beans, 6 cups of water and ham bone in a slow cooker, cover and cook on low for 8 hours. Feel free to add favorite spices and vegetables to this basic soup as it simmers.

HAWAIIAN RIBS

3 pounds of spareribs, trimmed
9 ounces of crushed pineapple, canned
½ cup of ketchup
¼ cup of vinegar
3 tablespoons of brown sugar
2 tablespoons of cornstarch
1 tablespoon of soy sauce
½ teaspoon of salt

Combine all the ingredients, except the ribs, in a pan. Stir the mixture and bring to a boil. Cook until thick, stirring frequently. Layer ribs in the crock pot and pour sauce over the meat. Cook on low for 6 to 8 hours.

HOMEMADE BAKED BEANS

2½ cups of Great Northern beans, dried
4 cups of water
1½ cups of tomato sauce
1 onion, diced
½ cup of brown sugar
2 teaspoons of salt
½ teaspoon of chili powder

Wash and drain beans. Put beans in the cooker with enough water to cover. Put on the lid and cook on low for 8 hours. Stir in remaining ingredients, cover and cook on low for 6 hours.

HUNTER'S CHICKEN

3 pounds of chicken parts
2 cloves of garlic
¼ cup of olive oil
1 small can of stewed tomatoes
1 onion, diced
¼ cup of sweet white wine
2 teaspoons or oregano
1 teaspoon of salt
1 teaspoon of paprika
½ teaspoon of basil
½ teaspoon of rosemary
Pepper to taste

In a pan, brown chicken parts with garlic in the olive oil. Put chicken in the cooker. Mix remaining ingredients together and pour over chicken. Cover and cook on low for 4 to 6 hours.

ITALIAN CHICKEN

1 chicken, in parts
1 can of cream of mushroom soup
1 package of dry Italian salad dressing mix
6 ounces of canned mushrooms, drained
Seasoning salt
Pepper to taste

Put chicken pieces in the cooker. Mix soup, salad dressing, seasoning salt and pepper and pour over meat. Top with mushrooms. Cover and cook on low for 4 to 6 hours.

ITALIAN PORK CHOPS

6 pork chops
16 ounces of tomato sauce
2 cans of green beans, French-cut
½ cup of green pepper, diced
1 onion, diced
1 clove of garlic, chopped
Oil
Water

Brown the pork chops in a skillet with a little oil. Place remaining ingredients in the cooker and stir. Put the pork chops on top of the ingredients. Pour in enough water to cover the chops. Cook on low for 6 to 8 hours.

JERKY CHILI

2½ cups of beef jerky
½ cup of chopped bacon
1 onion, chopped
2 cloves of garlic, minced
2 cups beef broth
4 chili peppers, chopped
2 tablespoons chili powder
2 tablespoons light brown sugar
1½ tablespoons of cumin
5 cups fresh tomatoes, peeled and chopped
½ tablespoon pepper
2 ½ cups kidney or pinto beans, cooked

Cook bacon in deep pot or Dutch oven until fat is released, but not crisp. Add onion and garlic and cook until tender. Add in chili peppers, tomatoes and broth. Cook until tomatoes are soft, 15 to 20 minutes. Now combine chili powder, brown sugar, cumin and pepper and then add to pot. Stir in the beef jerky. Simmer or low boil for 45 minutes. Add beans and boil for about 5 minutes.

KRAUT AND KIELBASA

1 pound of kielbasa, cut to bite-sized chunks
64 ounces of sauerkraut, canned or bagged
1 onion, diced
1 bay leaf

Combine all ingredients in the cooker. Add enough water to just cover ingredients. Cover then cook on high for 30 minutes then cook on low for 6 hours. Remove bay leaf before serving.

LAMB WITH HERBS

6 lamb shanks, cut in half
1 onion, sliced
1 cup of water
2 cloves of garlic, mashed
1 tablespoon of Worcestershire sauce
1 teaspoon of garlic salt
¼ teaspoon of marjoram
¼ teaspoon of thyme
¼ teaspoon of rosemary
¼ teaspoon of fresh ground pepper

Put lamb shanks in a cooker. Mix remaining ingredients together and pour over lamb. Cover and cook on low for 8 to 10 hours.

LAZY CHOPS

4 pork chops
1 can of cream of mushroom soup
¼ cup of ketchup
2 teaspoons of Worcestershire sauce

Place chops in the cooker. Combine remaining ingredients and pour over the meat. Cover and cook on low for 8 to 10 hours.

LOGGING CAMP STEW

2½ pounds of beef, cubed
½ pound of sliced mushrooms
28 ounces of canned tomatoes, crushed
3 cups of beef bouillon
1 cup of celery, diced
4 carrots, sliced
3 potatoes, diced large
3 tablespoons of flour
¼ cup of red wine
1 clove of garlic, crushed
10 ounces of peas, frozen
1 teaspoon of salt
1 teaspoon of pepper
1 teaspoon of Italian herbs
1 teaspoon of Kitchen Bouquet Browning and Seasoning Sauce (optional)

Put everything in a Dutch oven and mix together. Cover and bake at 250 degrees for 5 to 6 hours.

LOW & SLOW CHILI

2 pounds of ground beef, browned & drained
32 ounces of canned red kidney beans, drained
28 ounces of canned tomatoes, diced
2 medium onions, diced
2 cloves of garlic, minced
3 tablespoons of chili powder
1 teaspoon of cumin
1 teaspoon of black pepper
1 teaspoon of salt

Combine all the ingredients in the cooker. Cover and cook on low for 8 to 10 hours.

MEATLOAF

3 pounds of lean ground beef
½ pound of sausage, browned and drained
2 envelopes of dry onion soup mix
1 small can of evaporated milk
1 egg
1 onion, diced
Small potatoes

In a pan, cook and brown sausage in a pan and drain off the grease. Crumble the sausage and mix all of the ingredients into a loaf. Put meat in the cooker and place potatoes around the top. Cover and cook on low for 8 to 10 hours.

MEATLOAF II

2 pounds of lean ground beef
1 onion, diced
2 stalks of celery, diced
1½ cups of cooked rice
1 egg
2 tablespoons of mustard
½ cup of milk

Cook rice, white or wild, according to package directions. Mix all ingredients together and form into a loaf. Place in cooker, cover and cook on low for 8 to 10 hours.

ORCHARD SOUP

¼ cup of raisins
½ cup of dried prunes
½ cup of dried apples
½ cup of mixed, dried fruit
½ cup of Orange Tang
3 ounces or raspberry gelatin
1 cinnamon stick
½ cup of powdered whole milk
1 cup of hot water
Pinch of salt

Put dried fruits in a Dutch oven. Fill with dried fruits and cover with water. Stir in salt, Tang, gelatin and the cinnamon stick. Bring to a boil, cover and reduce to a simmer for 20 minutes or until fruit is tender. Stir dry milk into a cup of hot water until dissolved then add to fruit and thoroughly mix.

OYSTER STEW

20 fresh oysters in juice
1 stick of butter
1 cup of bottled clam juice
1 quart of half & half
¼ teaspoon of paprika
Cayenne pepper to taste
Celery salt to taste
Worcestershire sauce to taste

Put oysters and juice in cooker. Cover and cook on high until their edges curl slightly. Mix remaining ingredients together thoroughly and add to the oysters. Cook on low for 1 to 2 hours.

PEPPER CHICKEN

3 pounds of chicken parts
1 green pepper, diced large
8 ounces of canned water chestnuts, drained and sliced
¼ cup of soy sauce
3 tablespoons of water
2 teaspoons of cornstarch
½ teaspoon of salt

Remove skin and fat from the chicken parts. Put the pieces in the cooker. Combine soy sauce, salt and 1 tablespoon of water and pour it over the chicken. Cover and cook on medium for 90 minutes. Add water chestnuts and green pepper and cook for an additional 30 minutes. Mix cornstarch with 2 tablespoons of water. Stir into the cooker. Cook until thick, stirring constantly.

PHEASANT & MUSHROOMS

2 pheasants, cleaned and washed
1 can of cream of chicken or mushroom soup
1 onion, diced
4 ounces of mushrooms, sliced
½ cup of chicken broth
1 clove or garlic, minced
2 tablespoons of flour
1 tablespoon of Worcestershire sauce
1 teaspoon of salt
Paprika

Place birds in the cooker either whole or quartered. Mix all ingredients, except paprika and pour over the pheasants. Sprinkle with paprika. Cover and cook on low for 6 to 7 hours or until meat is tender.

PIZZA RICE

2 cups of rice, uncooked
3 cups of pizza sauce (thicker the better)
2½ cups of water
6 ounces of canned mushrooms with juice
4 ounces of pepperoni, sliced
1 cup of mozzarella cheese, shredded

Combine all the ingredients except the cheese, in the cooker. Cover and cook on low for 10 hours. Sprinkle with cheese just before serving.

PORK CHOPS & GRAVY

6 thick pork chops, trimmed of fat
2 cloves of garlic, mashed
1 can of cream of mushroom soup
1 can of mushrooms
1 can of tomato paste
Flour
Garlic salt
Salt and pepper to taste
Oil

Season flour with salt and pepper to taste. Dredge chops in the flour mixture. Put a little oil in a pan and brown chops. Put chops in the cooker. Mix together garlic, mushrooms, mushroom soup, and tomato paste with garlic salt, salt and pepper to taste. Pour mixture over chops in the cooker. Cover and cook on low for 8 to 10 hours.

PORK ROAST

3 pounds of pork tenderloin
16 ounces of canned cranberry sauce
1 sliced onion
1/3 cup of French dressing

Slice an onion and lay it on top of the meat. Mix cranberry sauce and dressing and smother the pork with the mixture. Cover and cook on low, about for 8 hours.

POT ROAST

3 pound roast (beef or venison)
2 cups of brewed coffee (not instant)
2 cans of cream of mushroom soup
1 package of dry Lipton Onion soup mix
Flour, salt and pepper

Flour and brown roast in a skillet. Mix remaining ingredients and put in crock-pot with roast. Cover and cook for 8 hours. Recipe works very well on tougher cuts of meat.

REFRIED BEAN DIP

20 ounces of refried beans
1 cup of Cheddar cheese, shredded
½ cup of green onions, diced
¼ teaspoon of salt
Taco sauce to taste

Combine all ingredients in the cooker. Cover and cook on low for 2½ hours. If you're in a hurry, cook on high for 30 minutes, than drop to low for 30 minutes.

RICE PUDDING

2½ cups of cooked rice
1½ cups of evaporated milk
3 eggs, beaten
¾ cup of rice, white or brown
¾ cup of raisin
3 tablespoons of butter
2 teaspoons of vanilla
1 teaspoon of nutmeg

Mix together all ingredients and pour into a lightly greased cooker. Cover and cook on low for 4 to 6 hours. After the first hour stir the pot.

SEAFOOD POT

1 pound of shrimp, peeled and de-veined
1 pound of crabmeat
1 pound of scallops
2 cans of cream of celery soup
2 soup cans of milk
2 tablespoons of melted butter
1 teaspoon of Old Bay seasoning
¼ teaspoon of salt
¼ teaspoon pepper

In the cooker layer shrimp, crab and scallops. Combine soup and milk and pour into the cooker. Mix butter with spices and pour over the top. Cover and cook on low for 3 to 4 hours.

SIMPLE CHICKEN

4 pounds of chicken pieces
(works great for wings)
½ cup of water
1 bottle of barbecue sauce (14 to 16 ounces)

Put water in the bottom of the cooker and add the chicken parts. Pour barbecue sauce over the meat. Cover and cook on low for 8 hours

SLOPPY CHICKEN

2 pounds of chicken, diced or shredded
16 ounces of chicken broth
1 can of cream of mushroom soup
1 can of cream of mushroom soup
1 sleeve of butter crackers, crushed

Combine all the ingredients in a cooker and cover. Cook on low for 5 to 6 hours and stir occasionally.

SLOW BURN BEANS

2½ pounds of canned great northern beans, drained
½ cup of catsup
½ cup of brown sugar
½ cup of molasses
1 tablespoon of mustard
1 onion, diced
1 teaspoon of salt
¼ teaspoon of ground ginger
1 pound of bacon, browned and crumbled

Brown bacon in a pan, drain the grease and crumble the strips. Put all ingredients in the cooker, cover and set on low. Cook for 4 hours.

SLOW POKE PORK

3 pounds of boneless pork roast, cubed
2 onions, diced
12 ounces of barbecue sauce
¼ cup of honey

Put meat in the cooker and add onions, honey and barbecue sauce. Cover and cook on low for 6 to 8 hours. When you pull out the meat, you can shred the pork with forks. Serve on rolls, hamburger buns on in a wrap.

SNOW DAY STEW

2 pounds of venison roast in 1-inch chunks
2 tablespoons of olive oil
2 cups of diced onions
2 cloves of garlic
4 cups of acorn squash, diced
1 cup of green onion, diced
1 cup of apple, diced
2 tablespoons of flour
1 teaspoon of cinnamon
1 tablespoon of ground cumin
¾ cup of apple cider
¾ cup of dark beer

In a pan, sauté venison, onions and garlic in the olive oil. Pour these ingredients into a slow cooker or Dutch oven. Cover and cook on low for 5 to 6 hours or until tender.

SOUTH OF THE BORDER BEANS

4 cans of kidney beans
2 onions, diced
2 cloves of garlic, minced
¼ cup of vinegar
2 tablespoons of sugar
1 stick of cinnamon
1 tablespoon of salt
1 tablespoon of dry mustard
3 tablespoons of chili powder
¼ teaspoon of cloves

Place ingredients in the cooker and stir. Cover and cook on low for 8 to 10 hours.

SPICED APPLE CIDER

1 gallon of apple cider
1 cup of orange juice
1 cup of sugar
½ cup of pineapple juice
2 cinnamon sticks
2 teaspoons of whole cloves
2 teaspoons of ground nutmeg
1 teaspoon of cinnamon
1 teaspoon of ground cloves
1 teaspoon of ginger
1 teaspoon of grated lemon zest

Mix all of the ingredients in the cooker, cover and cook on low for 4 to 6 hours. If batch is too large for your pot, halve all of the ingredients.

SPICY PORK CHOPS

6 pork chops
8 ounces of tomato sauce
1 onion, sliced
1 green pepper, sliced in strips
4 tablespoons of brown sugar
2 tablespoons of Worcestershire sauce
3 tablespoons of oil
1 tablespoon of vinegar
1½ teaspoons of salt

Brown pork chops in a pan with the oil then put meat in the cooker. Add remaining ingredients and cover. Cook on low for 6 to 8 hours.

TERIYAKI CHICKEN

3 pounds of skinless chicken pieces
20 ounces of pineapple chunks, canned
1 cup of teriyaki sauce
½ teaspoon of ground ginger

Place chicken in the cooker. Sprinkle ginger over the chicken, pour teriyaki in next and top with pineapple chunks. Cover and cook on low for 6 to 8 hours.

TROPICAL CHICKEN

3 whole chicken breasts cut in half
¼ cup of molasses
2 tablespoons of apple cider vinegar
2 tablespoon of Worcestershire sauce
2 tablespoons of orange juice
2 teaspoons of mustard
¼ teaspoon of hot sauce

Mix all the ingredients into a sauce. Place chicken in the cooker and pour on the sauce slowly. Cover and cook on low for 7 to 9 hours.

TUNA SALAD CASSEROLE

14 ounces of canned tuna
1 can of cream of celery soup
3 eggs, hard-boiled and diced
1 cup of diced celery
½ cup of mayonnaise or Miracle Whip
¼ teaspoon of fresh ground pepper
1½ cups of crushed potato chips

Combine the first 6 ingredients in the cooker. Top with potato chips. Cover the cooker and cook on low for 5 to 8 hours.

TURKEY BREAST BAKE

1 large, boneless turkey breast
¼ cup of apple cider or apple juice
1 teaspoon of salt
½ teaspoon of pepper

Put turkey in the cooker and drizzle with apple cider/juice. Sprinkle salt and pepper on top and bottom of the breast. Cover and cook on high for 3 to 4 hours. When cooking is done, let breast stand for 10 minutes before slicing.

TURKEY CHILI

1 pound of ground turkey
3 pounds of red beans, canned with liquid
1 cup of corn, frozen
1 onion, diced
6 ounces of tomato paste
3 teaspoon of chili powder
3 tablespoons of oil
½ teaspoon of salt

Sauté onion in a pan until it turns transparent. Add turkey and salt and brown lightly. Combine all ingredients in a slow cooker and mix well. Cover and cook on low for 8 to 9 hours.

TURKEY STEW

2 pounds of skinless turkey thighs
15 ounces of tomato sauce
1 pound of carrots, sliced
2 onions, diced
7 potatoes, cubed
4 stalks of celery, diced
3 cloves of garlic, minced
1 teaspoon of salt
2 tablespoons of Worcestershire sauce
2 bay leaves

Place the turkey in the cooker. In a bowl, mix carrots, onions, potatoes, celery, garlic, salt, pepper, Worcestershire sauce, tomato sauce and bay leaves. Pour mixture over the turkey. Cover and cook on low for 8 to 12 hours. Remove bay leaves before serving.

VEGETABLE BEEF SOUP

1 pound of beef, cubed
1 cup of beef bouillon
1½ cups of cabbage, shredded
1½ cups of stewed tomatoes, undrained
1½ cups of corn, frozen or canned
1½ cups of frozen peas
1½ cups of frozen green beans
1½ cups of carrots, sliced
½ teaspoon of salt

Put all ingredients in a cooker. Cover and cook on low for 6 to 8 hours.

VENISON CHILI

2 pounds of ground venison
¼ cup cooking oil
1 cup chopped onion
2 cloves garlic, minced
1 large green pepper, chopped
3 tablespoons chili powder
2 cups tomatoes
1 cup of tomato sauce
1 cup of water
½ teaspoon salt
3 cups cooked kidney beans
1 tablespoon of flour mixed
with 2 tablespoons of water

Brown venison in oil in a deep pot or Dutch oven until meat loses pink color. Add onion, garlic and green pepper and cook for an additional 5 minutes. Stir in chili powder, tomatoes, tomato sauce, water and salt. Cover and simmer for 2 hours. Add flour paste and cook until mixture thickens. Stir in kidney beans and cook for another 15 minutes.

WHOLE WHEAT & CORNMEAL BREAD

1½ cups of buttermilk
1 cup of whole-wheat flour
1 cup of cornmeal
½ cup of dark molasses
1 teaspoon of baking powder
1 teaspoon of baking soda
½ teaspoon of salt
1 cup of nuts, chopped (optional)
1 cup of raisins (optional)

Make a batter with all of the ingredients. Pour the batter into a greased and floured clean, coffee or similar metal container. Make sure the can that fits loosely in the cooker. The batter should only fill 2/3 of the can. Cover can top tightly with aluminum foil. Put can in the cooker. Pour in enough water into the cooker so that it's filled to ½-inch from the top. Put foil over the cooker and then put the lid on. Cook on high for 4 hours.

WINE & CRANBERRY PUNCH

1 pint of cranberry juice cocktail
1 cup of water
¾ cup of sugar
2 cinnamon sticks
6 whole cloves
1 gallon of burgundy wine
1 lemon, thinly sliced

Combine all ingredients in the cooker. Cover and heat on low for 90 minutes. Strain and serve. If this recipe is too much for your cooker to hold, cut all of the ingredients in half.

WITCHES CAULDRON STEW

1 pound of bacon, chopped and uncooked
1 pound of lean ground beef
30 ounces of kidney beans, canned
28 ounces of canned tomatoes with juice
10 ounces of mushrooms, canned
2 cups of uncooked egg noodles
1 cup of celery, diced
1 cup of onion, diced
2 cloves of garlic, minced
1 teaspoon of pepper
1 teaspoon of seasoned salt
1 teaspoon of cayenne pepper

Brown bacon, hamburger and onion in a Dutch oven and drain the fat. Add celery, onion, tomatoes, beans, noodles and mushrooms plus liquid from the cans. Add seasoning and stir. Bake at 350 degrees for 45 minutes.

WORTH-THE-WAIT BEEF STEW

2 pounds of beef, cut into 1½-inch cubes
6 carrots, sliced
6 small boiling onions, whole
4 stalks of celery, diced
4 cups of boiling water
½ cup of flour
3 tablespoons of shortening
1 onion, sliced
1 clove of garlic
1 teaspoon of salt
1 teaspoon of sugar
1 teaspoon of lemon juice
1 teaspoon of Worcestershire sauce
½ teaspoon of pepper
½ teaspoon of paprika
1/8 teaspoon of cloves

Dredge meat in flour. Melt shortening in the Dutch oven. Add beef slowly and sauté until browned. Keep pieces from touching. Add in all other ingredients except vegetables and stir. Cover and cook over low heat for 2 to 3 hours. Add vegetables and cook for an additional 30 minutes or until vegetables are tender.

For more information on the entire series of Tim Murphy's "Cookbooks for Guys" and his other book projects, visit www.flanneljohn.com.